Christ in You

Introductory Bible Studies
on Christian Living

Second edition © 1979 by Inter-Varsity Christian Fellowship of the United States of America. First edition © 1956 by Inter-Varsity Christian Fellowship of the United States of America.

All rights reserved. No part of this booklet may be reproduced in any form without written permission from InterVarsity Press, Downers Grove, Illinois.

InterVarsity Press is the book-publishing division of Inter-Varsity Christian Fellowship, a student movement active on campus at hundreds of universities, colleges and schools of nursing. For information about local and regional activities, write IVCF, 233 Langdon St., Madison, WI 53703.

ISBN 0-87784-175-6

Printed in the United States of America

21	20	19	18	17	16	15	14	13	12	11
07	06	05	04	03	02	01	00	99	98	97

Christianity is Christ. Christians are people who are in vital contact with God because Jesus Christ is living in them. Christ is their life and strength. It is only through him that they are able to live a life pleasing to God.

If you are now a Christian, it can really be said that Christ is in you (Colossians 1:27). To grow and mature in your Christianity is to have the characteristics of Jesus Christ more and more prominent in your daily life. This process takes place as the person and work of Christ become more meaningful to you.

God has provided in the Bible a revelation of himself and his working in human history. The Old Testament gives us an account of his dealings with people through the centuries before Christ came to earth. In the New Testament we have a record of the life and teachings of Jesus, his death on the cross for our sins and his resurrection. There is also an account of how the early Christians grew in their faith as they were led by the Holy Spirit. It is essential that we study the Scriptures. As the Word of God lives in our hearts and is worked out in our lives, we become fruitful disciples.

This booklet is designed to help you as a young Christian start studying the Bible for yourself. It deals with basic, practical questions which all Christians encounter as they mature. The first two sections concern Jesus Christ as our living Lord and the assurance of eternal life which we have in him. Then follows a chapter on the basic principles of Christian living. Chapter four considers relations among Christians as members of the body of Christ. The last two chapters deal with the problems of temptation and of becoming fruitful disciples. Finally there is a brief section which presents the underlying motive in the Christian life.

Your first step is to choose a translation of the Bible. The King James Version is sometimes difficult to understand. And while paraphrases may be helpful in reading the Bible, they are not recommended for serious study because of the many liberties taken in producing them. You should get a reliable modern translation—at least of the New Testament—to aid your study.

Each chapter of this booklet is divided into a number of sections. Since careful study is important, it might be best at the start to do only one section at a sitting. A brief time spent regularly each day will be of more value than longer periods taken less frequently.

There is nothing sacred about this booklet nor is there any intrinsic merit in answering questions. But you will find it valuable to study the teaching of the Bible concerning these basic subjects. Writing the answers in your own words in the space provided will help you to understand the Scripture and retain what you learn. Using this booklet should prepare you for continued personal study of the Bible.

The Christian life is not necessarily an easy one; don't think that your troubles ceased the moment you received Christ. In certain ways they increased, but the great difference is that now you have a Lord who understands you perfectly and has the answers to all your problems. God in his grace has provided a full and complete salvation in his Son.

Christ in you offers you the strength to serve God and live a life of abundant joy. This life is for the person who says with Paul, "It is no longer I who live, but Christ who lives in me; and the life I now live in the flesh I live by faith in the Son of God, who loved me and gave himself for me" (Galatians 2:20).

1
Jesus Christ, Our Living Lord

Before answering any of the questions, read the short passage through. Then look for the answers to the specific questions in the verses in parentheses.

I Jesus Christ: The Person
1. Read Hebrews 1:1-4. How has God revealed himself (vv. 1-2)?
2. What characteristics and actions of the Son make God's revelation through him unique (vv. 2-3)?
3. What has Jesus Christ done for you (v. 3)?

II Jesus Christ: Our Life
1. Read Colossians 3:1-5, 12-14, 23-24. What changed attitude should you have as a Christian? Why (vv. 1-2)?
2. In what sense have you died and been raised with Christ (vv. 1, 3)? See also Romans 6:8-11.
3. Write down any practical differences it will make to you that Christ is "our life" (vv. 4-5, 12-14).
4. What new allegiance do you now have as a

Christian? How will it motivate you in your activities today (vv. 23-24)?

Thought question: Try to imagine that Jesus Christ had not risen from the dead. What difference does it make in your life that you are serving a risen Lord and not just a dead martyr?

III Jesus Christ: In You

1. Read John 14:15-26. Jesus Christ spoke these words to his disciples just before his death. He wanted them to know that he was leaving them only temporarily and that he would return to live with them in another way.

Who is the Spirit, and what part does he play in revealing Christ and the Father to you (vv. 16-17, 26)? (Note the personal pronoun *he* in these verses.)

2. What makes the relationship between Christ and Christians so close (vv. 16-20)?

3. Why is it that Jesus Christ is known personally to his followers and not to the whole world (vv. 22-24)?

4. Read Ephesians 3:14-19. What is God's purpose for you as a Christian (vv. 17-19)?

5. How is this accomplished (v. 16)?

2
Assurance of Eternal Life

I Our Changed Condition
1. Read Romans 5:1-11. What was the condition of humanity that caused God to send his Son to die for us (vv. 6, 8, 10)?
2. What new relationship to God do you have through Christ's death and life (vv. 1-2, 9-11)?
3. Read Hebrews 7:23-27. In your own words state how it is that Christ is able to save us for all time (vv. 24-26).
4. What assurance do you have that your sins have been completely forgiven (v. 27)? See also Hebrews 9:25-26.
5. Read John 3:16-18. What has God made possible for the world through the gift of his Son (vv. 16-17)?
6. How can you be sure you will not be condemned (vv. 17-18)? See also Jesus' words in John 5:24.

II Our Changing Character
1. Read 1 John 2:1-6. How can you be sure that

you will not be abandoned by God if you should sin (vv. 1-2)? Note John's use of *Father*.

2. On the other hand, what indication do you find here that the Christian is not free to continue to disobey God (vv. 3-4)?

3. What evidence should there be in your life that you truly know Jesus Christ and abide in him (vv. 3, 5-6)?

III Our Changeless Confidence

1. Read Romans 8:31-39. How can you know that God loves you (vv. 31-32)?

2. Find actions and aspects of Jesus Christ which assure you of no condemnation (vv. 33-34).

3. What confidence can you have as you face any of the perils referred to in verses 35-39?

4. Read Hebrews 10:21-23. Since you have such a complete salvation through Jesus Christ, what should your response be?

3
Abiding in Christ

I Our Personal Relationship with Christ
1. Read John 15:1-11. Our Lord Jesus Christ here teaches clearly the way in which your new life develops. First read the entire passage carefully.

What is the nature of the relationship between Christ and you (vv. 1-2, 4-5)?
2. What are the results of abiding in Christ (vv. 5, 7-8)?
3. Very practically, what is involved in having Christ abiding in you and in your abiding in him (vv. 7, 10)?

II The Word of God
1. Read John 5:37-40. Here Jesus is responding to the challenges of the religious leaders of his day. For what did Christ criticize them? Therefore, what ought to be the aim of your Bible study?
2. Read 2 Timothy 3:14-17. For what purposes has God given us the Holy Scriptures (vv. 15-17)?
3. What must you do if these purposes are to be accomplished (vv. 14-15)? See also James 1:22-25.

4. Read 1 Corinthians 2:12-16. Why can you not expect to understand or accept God's truth by human intelligence alone? Are you depending on your own wisdom to understand the Bible (v. 14)?

5. What provision has God made to help you understand the spiritual truths in his Word (vv. 12, 16)?

III Prayer

Some of the most profound illustrations of prayer may be found in the book of Psalms. Carefully read Psalm 27. From studying this psalm you will be able to see how the rest of the book can be an inspiring guide to prayer.

1. What is the great desire of the psalmist in prayer (vv. 4, 8)?

2. What characterizes the psalmist's attitude toward God in prayer?

3. What specific prayer of your own does this psalm suggest to you? Make this your prayer now.

4. Read John 14:13-14. What important role does Jesus Christ have as you pray (vv. 13-14)? See also John 15:7.

5. For what purpose does God answer specific prayer requests (v. 13)? See also John 15:8.

4
Living in Fellowship

As a Christian, you do not stand alone. Since through Jesus Christ you have become a child of God (John 1:12), you have a definite relationship to all other Christians.

I The Body of Christ

1. Read Ephesians 4:1-16. How are Christians related to each other and what is the basis of their unity (vv. 4-6)?
2. Very practically, what are you to do to help keep this unity (vv. 1-3)?
3. What picture is given of the relationship of Christians to their Lord (vv. 12, 15-16)?
4. What provision has God made for building up the church (vv. 7-8, 11-12)? See also 1 Corinthians 12:27-28 and Romans 12:4-8.
5. State in your own words the goal of Christian fellowship (vv. 13-16).

II The Local Church

1. While all Christians are members of the church

universal, those living in one locality meet together to become a local church (1 Corinthians 1:2).

Read Acts 2:41-47. In this example of the fellowship of early Christians, find the important functions of a local church. See also 1 Corinthians 11:23-26.

2. What promise has Jesus Christ made for such a gathering (Matthew 18:20)?

3. What other reasons are given in Hebrews 10: 23-25 for meeting together? What error were some Christians making? Are you doing the same?

III Love in Action

1. Read 1 Corinthians 12:14-26. Why does God give Christians different capabilities (vv. 14, 17-20)?

2. In view of this fact, what should be your attitude toward those with differing functions (vv. 21-25)?

3. How is your life interrelated with other Christians (v. 26)?

4. Read 1 John 3:14-18. By what characteristic is a Christian fellowship to be known (v. 14)?

5. In what practical ways can you love others as Christ has loved you?

5
Facing Sin and Temptation

I The Source of Sin
1. Read James 1:12-15. Why should you never think you are tempted by God (v. 13)?
2. What is the real source of temptation (v. 14)?
3. What is the difference between temptation and sin (vv. 14-15)?

II Help and Comfort in Temptation
1. Read Hebrews 4:14-16. Why is it that Christ is able to sympathize with us in our times of temptation (v. 15)?
2. How does Jesus Christ's experience described in Matthew 4:1-11 illustrate this fact? What different types of temptation did he endure?
3. Since you have such a sympathetic high priest, what should you do in time of temptation (v. 16)? See also God's promise in 1 Corinthians 10:13.
4. Write God's promise in 1 Corinthians 10:13 in your own words.

III Avoiding Temptation

The following verses give you practical suggestions for avoiding temptation. Write the suggestion given in each passage in your own words.

Matthew 26:41.
2 Timothy 2:22.
James 4:7.
Ephesians 6:10-18.
Philippians 4:8.

IV Victory over Sin

1. Read 1 John 5:1-5. What should be our motive for not sinning against God (vv. 2-3)?

2. Who can overcome anything in the world (vv. 4-5)?

3. Why is it possible for you who believe in Christ to overcome the world? See also John 16:33.

4. What provision has God made for you when you do sin (Psalm 32:5; 1 John 1:9)? What is your responsibility in the matter?

6
Becoming Fruitful Disciples

I Christ's Life in Us
1. Read Galatians 2:20. What is it that makes you "alive" as a Christian? How do you stay "alive"?
2. Read Galatians 5:13-26 looking for how Christ actually lives in me. By what characteristics does this aliveness show itself (vv. 22-23, 25)? How do these characteristics also describe Jesus Christ?
3. What resistance to this fruitful life will you encounter? How do you account for this recurrent tendency to do wrong (vv. 16-17)?
4. Which "works of the flesh" do you notice in your own life? Are any others potential (vv. 19-21)?
5. Who helps you to be victorious in this conflict, and how do you cooperate (vv. 16, 25-26)?
6. How is this life of Christ in you to be apparent and expressed to others (vv. 13-14)?

II Making Christ Known
1. Read Philippians 2:12-16. What do you learn from Paul about the relationship between God's work and yours in Christian living and witness (vv. 12-13)? See also Colossians 1:27-29.

2. What is your responsibility as you live among people who do not know Christ (vv. 14-16)?

3. Read Matthew 28:18-20. What final commission did the Lord give to his disciples?

4. What promise from Christ may you claim when you feel inadequate as a witness (vv. 18, 20)?

5. Read 2 Corinthians 5:14-21. What is the compelling motivation in presenting Christ (vv. 14-15)?

6. Summarize briefly in your own words the message which has been entrusted to you (vv. 17-21).

III Christ as a Witness

1. In Revelation 1:5 Jesus is called the "faithful witness." Read John 4:4-26 to see how you can introduce others to him. What ordinary experience did Jesus use for witnessing (vv. 7-9)? What natural opportunities do you have to speak of Christ?

2. Note that Jesus avoided an argument about religious opinions (vv. 19-24). What main point does this emphasize about your own witness?

3. Observe Jesus' attitude toward the woman. What characteristics of a good witness do you find?

4. Notice how enthusiastically the woman told others what little she knew about Christ. What have you learned from your experience with the Lord Jesus Christ that you want to share with others?

The Pursuit of Christ

As in friendships on the human level, a Christian's relationship with his or her Lord is one of having found yet still seeking. It is well expressed in the hymn of Bernard of Clairvaux:

> We taste Thee, O Thou Living Bread,
>   And long to feast upon Thee still;
> We drink of Thee, the Fountain-Head,
>   And thirst our souls from Thee to fill.

In the New Testament Paul is the outstanding example of a person dominated by love for Jesus Christ. He combined the assurance of "I know whom I have believed" (2 Timothy 1:12) and the seeking prayer "that I may know him" (Philippians 3:10). Having found Jesus Christ, he channeled all his energy into knowing him better and making him known.

Read carefully Philippians 3:7-14 and then write down in your own words what Jesus Christ means to you and what you see as your purpose in life.

for further study from InterVarsity Press

Quiet Time
This guidebook suggests practical methods for beginning and maintaining a daily time of Bible study and prayer. paper, 30 pages

Basic Christianity
John R. W. Stott sets forth a clear statement of the fundamental content of Christianity. Excellent for seekers and believers. paper, 142 pages

Grow Your Christian Life
These twelve weeks of daily Bible study cover such topics as personal evangelism, sin, knowing God's will, prayer and marriage. paper, 84 studies

The Fight
John White looks at the basic areas of the Christian life—faith, fellowship, Bible study, guidance and others; here are profound insights to the joys and struggles of life in Christ. paper, 230 pages